Acknowledgements

For permission to reprint the passages quoted in this book, we are indebted to:

W.H. Allen & Co. Ltd and Alan Sillitoe for the extract from *The Loneliness of the Long Distance Runner*

Angus & Robertson (UK) Ltd and Ivan Southall for the extract from *To the Wild Sky*

Edward Arnold (Publishers) Ltd and J. Meade Falkner for the extract from *Moonfleet*

The Estate of the late H.E. Bates for the extract from *Fair Stood the Wind for France*, published by Michael Joseph Ltd

The Bodley Head for the extracts from *The Great Gatsby* by F. Scott Fitzgerald and *The Gun* by C.S. Forester; and also to E.R. Braithwaite for the extract from *To Sir with Love*

Chatto & Windus Ltd and the Literary Estate of Richard Hughes for the extract from *A High Wind in Jamaica*

John Christopher for the extract from *The Death of Grass*, published by Michael Joseph Ltd

Rex Collings Ltd, London, and Richard Adams for the extract from *Watership Down*

Constable & Co. Ltd and Leslie Thomas for the extract from *This Time Next Week*

André Deutsch Ltd and Jack Schaefer for the extract from *Shane*

Faber & Faber Ltd and William Golding for the extract from *Lord of the Flies*

Victor Gollancz Ltd and D.R. Sherman for the extract from *Old Mali and the Boy*; also to: Alexander Solzhenitsyn for the extract from *One Day in the Life of Ivan Denisovich*; and to John le Carré for the extract from *The Spy Who Came in from the Cold* (both published by Victor Gollancz Ltd)

Granada Publishing Ltd and Gerald Durrell for the extract from *My Family and Other Animals*

Hamish Hamilton Ltd and L.P. Hartley for the extract from *The Go-Between*

William Heinemann Ltd, The Bodley Head and Graham Greene for the extract from *Brighton Rock*; also to William Heinemann Ltd for the extracts from *Of Mice and Men* by John Steinbeck and *To Kill a Mockingbird* by Harper Lee

The Executors of the Ernest Hemingway Estate for the extract from *The Old Man and the Sea*, published by Jonathan Cape Ltd

John Hersey for the extract from *Hiroshima*, published by Hamish Hamilton Ltd, Copyright © John Hersey, 1946, 1966

Hodder & Stoughton Ltd for the extract from *Everest South West Face* by Chris Bonington, Copyright © British Everest Expedition (1972) Partnership 1973

The Hogarth Press Ltd and Laurie Lee for the extract from *Cider with Rosie*

Hutchinson Publishing Group Ltd for the extract from *At One with the Sea* by Naomi James and *The Member of the Wedding* by Carson McCullers, published by Cresset Press

Mrs Laura Huxley and Chatto & Windus Ltd for the extract from *Brave New World* by Aldous Huxley

Michael Joseph Ltd for the extract from *The Chrysalids* by John Wyndham; also to: Stan Barstow for the extract from *Joby*; Barry Hines for the extract from *A Kestrel for a Knave*; James Vance Marshall for the extract from *Walkabout*; and Keith Waterhouse for the extract from *Billy Liar* (all published by Michael Joseph Ltd)

The Executors of the James Joyce Estate for the extract from *A Portrait of the Artist as a Young Man*, published by Jonathan Cape Ltd

Daphne du Maurier for the extract from *Jamaica Inn*, published by Victor Gollancz Ltd

Methuen & Co. Ltd for the extract from *The Card* by Arnold Bennett

The Estate of the late Nicholas Monsarrat for the extract from *The Cruel Sea*, published by Cassell Ltd

Mrs Sonia Brownell Orwell and Martin Secker & Warburg Ltd for the extract from *Animal Farm* by George Orwell

A.D. Peters & Co. Ltd and Ray Bradbury for the extract from *Fahrenheit 451*, published by Rupert Hart-Davis [Hart-Davis, MacGibbon]

Charles Portis for the extract from *True Grit*, published by Jonathan Cape Ltd

Vallentine Mitchell & Co. Ltd, London, for the extract from *The Diary of Anne Frank*

A.P. Watt Ltd for the extracts from *The Thirty-nine Steps* by John Buchan and from *A Town Like Alice* by Nevil Shute

Passages for Comprehension

PETER CLOKE

Head of English, Hele's School, Exeter

Wheaton

A Division of Pergamon Press

A. Wheaton & Company Limited
A Division of Pergamon Press
Hennock Road, Exeter EX2 8RP

Pergamon Press Ltd
Headington Hill Hall, Oxford OX3 0BW

Pergamon Press Inc.
Maxwell House, Fairview Park, Elmsford, New York 10523

Pergamon of Canada Ltd
Suite 104, 150 Consumers Road, Willowdale, Ontario M2J 1P9

Pergamon Press (Australia) Pty Ltd
P.O. Box 544, Potts Point, N.S.W. 2011

Pergamon Press GmbH
6242 Kronberg/Taunus, Pferdstrasse 1, Frankfurt-am-Main,
Federal Republic of Germany

First published in Great Britain 1980

Printed in Great Britain by A. Wheaton & Co. Ltd, Exeter

ISBN 0 08 025606 6

Contents

The aim of *Passages for Comprehension* is to introduce pupils in the 11–15 age group to a wide range of significant novels and to give them practice in basic comprehension skills. Most of the extracts are taken from books which have appeared in C.S.E. or O-level syllabuses in recent years and include fiction, non-fiction and autobiography.

Each of the fifty extracts is followed by ten questions which examine the pupils' understanding of the main facts and events in the passage. At least two of these questions are inferential in nature and invite a longer written answer.

EXERCISE 1   Hunting the Pig

The bushes crashed ahead of them. Boys flung themselves wildly from the pig track and scrabbled in the creepers, screaming. Ralph saw Jack nudged aside and fall. Then there was a creature bounding along the pig track towards him, with tusks gleaming and an intimidating grunt. Ralph found he was able to measure the distance coldly and take aim. With the boar only five yards away, he flung the foolish wooden stick that he carried, saw it hit the great snout and hang there for a moment. The boar's note changed to a squeal and it swerved aside into the covert. The pig-run filled with shouting boys again, Jack came running back and poked about in the undergrowth.

William Golding, *Lord of the Flies*

1   How did the boys know that the boar was charging towards them?
2   What did the boys do to avoid the pig?
3   What happened to Jack?
4   How far away was the boar when Jack threw his stick?
5   Where did the stick strike the boar?
6   What did the boar do when the stick fell off?
7   What did the boys do when the boar had gone?
8   Why do you think Ralph did not panic?
9   Why was the boar so frightening?
10 What might Jack be looking for in the undergrowth?

1

EXERCISE 2 — A Strange Meeting

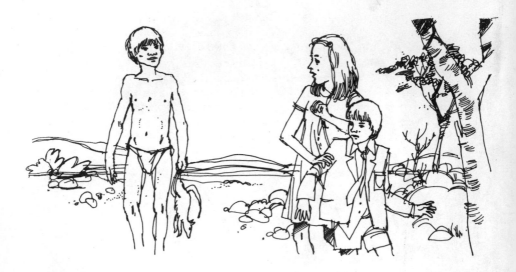

The girl's first impulse was to grab Peter and run; but as her eyes swept over the stranger, her fear died slowly. The boy was young – certainly no older than she was; he was unarmed, and his attitude was more inquisitive than threatening: more puzzled than hostile.

He wasn't the least bit like an African Negro. His skin was certainly black, but beneath it was a curious hint of undersurface bronze, and it was fine grained: glossy, satiny, almost silk-like. His hair wasn't crinkly but nearly straight; and his eyes were blue black: big, soft and inquiring. In his hand was a baby wallaby, its eyes, unclosed in death, staring vacantly above a tiny pointed snout.

James Vance Marshall, *Walkabout*

1 What did the girl want to do as soon as she saw the stranger? *grab Peter and*
2 What did she notice about the boy's age? *Young.*
3 What did the boy's skin look like? *black/bronze.*
4 What was so striking about the boy's eyes? *big black soft and inquiring*
5 What was the boy holding in his hand? *baby wallaby*
6 How was the boy's hair different from that of an African Negro? *nearly st*
7 What was so noticeable about the wallaby's eyes? *vacant*
8 Where might this strange meeting have taken place? *outback*
9 How might the boy have caught the wallaby? *in a trap.*
10 What do you think the boy thought of Peter and the girl? *Why were they*

2

EXERCISE 3 Big and Beautiful

When at last the gun reached the road the regiment eyed it and its escort with curiosity. The gun was huge, enormous in their eyes, accustomed to the little six-pounders which were all the Spanish army could boast nowadays. It came crashing and clattering down the road on its vast five-foot wheels with a most intoxicating noise. The odd team which drew it – three mules, six asses and a couple of cows – did not appear so strange; they were used to seeing the military train drawn by assorted teams. And the men who came with it were not so unusual a spectacle either; they had often seen guerillo bands before and more than half of them had been guerillos before they had been caught and clapped into the ranks of the army.

C.S. Forester, *The Gun*

1 Why did the gun appear to be so huge?
2 How big were the gun-carriage wheels?
3 How was the gun being pulled along?
4 Why do you think such an odd team was being used?
5 Why did this team not appear strange to the onlookers?
6 What sort of noises did the gun make as it was being pulled along?
7 Who was escorting the gun?
8 Why did their appearance not surprise the regiment?
9 How many members of the army had been guerillos before joining up?
10 Why do you think such a huge gun was needed?

EXERCISE 4 The Flooded Crypt

It was plain enough that the whole place had been under water: the floor was still muddy, and the green and sweating walls showed the flood-mark within two feet of the roof; there was a wisp or two of fine seaweed that had somehow got in and a small crab was still alive and scuttled across the corner, yet the coffins were but little disturbed. They lay on the shelves in rows, one above the other, and numbered twenty-three in all: most were in lead, and so could never float, but of those in wood some were turned slantways in their niches, and one had floated right away and been left on the floor upside-down in a corner when the waters went back.

J. Meade Falkner, *Moonfleet*

1 How could you tell from the condition of the floor that the place had been flooded?
2 How high up the walls had the water reached?
3 How had the water affected the walls?
4 What other signs of flooding by sea water were noticeable?
5 How many coffins were there?
6 Where were they kept?
7 Why had most of the coffins not been moved by the water?
8 What had happened to the wooden coffins?
9 Where do you think this 'place' might be?
10 Can you think of any reasons why the story-teller happened to be there?

EXERCISE 5 Packing Up

They picked up the gear from the boat. The old man carried the mast on his shoulder and the boy carried the wooden box with the coiled, hard-braided brown lines, the gaff and the harpoon with its shaft. The box with the baits was under the stern of the skiff along with the club that was used to subdue the big fish when they were brought alongside. No one would steal from the old man but it was better to take the sail and the heavy lines home as the dew was bad for them and, although he was quite sure no local people would steal from him, the old man thought that a gaff and a harpoon were needless temptations to leave in a boat.

Ernest Hemingway, *The Old Man and the Sea*

4

1 How did the old man carry the mast?
2 What was in the wooden box?
3 What was the club, kept in the stern of the boat, used for?
4 What else was kept there?
5 Why did they take the sail and heavy lines home with them?
6 Why did the old man not leave the gaff and harpoon in the skiff?
7 What colour were the fishing lines?
8 What sort of fish do you think the old man tried to catch?
9 Why do you think no one would try to steal from the old man?
10 Why might the boy have sought the friendship of the old man and helped him in this way?

EXERCISE 6 *The Unwanted Visitor*

He thought afterwards that the woman must have seen him from the windows. She came running out of the house and then stopped very suddenly, about five yards from him, her body flattened upright by the act of stopping, her hands slightly uplifted. All the time they were speaking she did not come any nearer.

'I'm English,' he said.

He felt foolish. His French, normally very fair, would not come. He stood looking at her stupidly. She was a little woman, about sixty, her hair drawn tightly back in a grey knot, her yellow brown face scared and almost hostile.

'No,' she said. 'No. Not here. Not here.'.

'Something to eat,' he said.

'No.' she stood arrested, more scared than himself, her very dark eyes staring.

H.E. Bates, *Fair Stood the Wind for France*

1 Where had the woman been standing when she had first seen the man?
2 How far away from the old man did the woman stop?
3 Why did she not come any nearer?
4 Why did the man feel so foolish?
5 How old was the woman?
6 What did her hair look like?
7 What did the man want?
8 What expression did the woman have on her face as she refused to give the man what he wanted?
9 Why do you think the woman was so frightened of the man?
10 How do you think the man came to be in this situation?

EXERCISE 7 Journey by Mule

Immediately the mule began to trot the Countess began to smile again. Relief and content were painted upon her handsome features. Denry soon learnt that she knew all about mules – or almost all. She told him how she had ridden hundreds of miles on mules in the Appenines, where there were no roads, and only mules, goats, and flies could keep their feet on the steep, stony paths. She said that a good mule was worth forty pounds in the Appenines, more than a horse of similar quality. In fact, she was very sympathetic about mules. Denry saw that he must drive with as much style as possible, and he tried to remember all that he had picked up from a book concerning the proper manner of holding the reins.

Arnold Bennett, *The Card*

1 When did the Countess begin to smile again?
2 What were conditions like in the Appenines?
3 How much was a good mule worth there?
4 Why was a mule more valuable than a horse in this part of the country?
5 What did a mule have in common with the goats and flies?
6 How had Denry learned to ride a mule?
7 Why do you think he was so anxious to impress the Countess?
8 Why do you think the Countess was so relieved when the mule began to trot?
9 What do you think might be the purpose of their expedition?
10 Do you think that the Countess will be taken in by Denry's attempts to cover up his lack of experience?

EXERCISE 8 The Raids

Occasional small raids used to happen two or three times a year, and nobody took much notice of them as a rule – except the people who got raided, of course, Usually they had time to get away and lost only their stock. Then everybody would contribute a little in kind, or in money, to help them set up again. But as time went on and the frontier was pushed back there were more Fringes people trying to live on less country. Some years they got very hungry, and after a time it was no longer just a matter of a dozen or so making a quick raid and then running back into Fringes country; they came instead in large organized bands and did a lot of damage.

John Wyndham, *The Chrysalids*

1　Why did people not take much notice of the early raids?
2　How many raiders usually took part in these raids?
3　How often did these raids take place?
4　Where did the raiders come from?
5　What did they usually steal?
6　How were the victims helped after the raids?
7　Why did the people of the Fringes begin to get very hungry?
8　How did the pattern of the raids change?
9　Why do you think the frontiers would have been pushed back?
10　How might the farmers have prevented the raids from happening?

EXERCISE 9　$\mathcal{A}$ Happy Farewell

I left Moor House at three o'clock p.m., and soon after four I stood at the foot of the sign-post of Whitecross, waiting the arrival of the coach which was to take me to distant Thornfield. Amidst the silence of those solitary roads and desert hills, I heard it approach from a great distance. It was the same vehicle whence, a year ago, I had alighted one summer evening on this very spot – how desolate, and hopeless, and objectless! It stopped as I beckoned. I entered – not now obliged to part with my whole fortune as the price of its accommodation. Once more on the road to Thornfield, I felt like the messenger-pigeon flying home.

Charlotte Brontë, *Jane Eyre*

1 What time did the girl leave Moor House? *3:00*
2 How long did it take her to reach the sign-post at Whitecross? *1 hour*
3 What was the girl waiting for? *coach*
4 Why was the girl able to hear the coach coming from a long way off? *silence*
5 Why did the coach look familiar? *she had used it a year before.*
6 How did the girl stop the coach? *beamed*
7 How did the girl feel now that she was returning to Thornfield? *messenger ?*
8 How do we know that the girl's luck has improved during the past year? *cheape*
9 How do you think the girl felt as she waited at the signpost?
10 Why had the girl been sent to Moor House for a year? *work.*

EXERCISE 10 *Mid-air Crisis*

Jim couldn't be sick. He was a strong man. He had marked up thousands of hours in the air; he'd been a pilot of light aircraft for more than twenty years. He had flown in North America and the Antarctic and in Africa. Men like Jim didn't get sick in the air.

The aircraft was slipping; it was beginning to lose height; beginning to go down in a wide and curious curve; and Jan was waking up, struggling under the weight that bore against her. Gerald saw her face twisting and straining, and knew that she was crying out, shouting; he could see that she could not dislodge Jim and that he seemed to be incapable of raising himself.

Gerald's mental block was still there, his panic was still there, and his fear of crossing the aircraft's centre of gravity was also there. He knew that if he moved forward the angle of dive must also inevitably steepen. If he transferred his own weight forward he might never shift Jim from the controls. The dive might become too steep.

Ivan Southall, *To the Wild Sky*

1   How long had Jim been a pilot?
2   What type of aircraft did he usually fly?
3   In which parts of the world had he gained his flying experience?
4   Why was it so difficult to believe that Jim could be ill?
5   What happened to the aircraft as it began to lose height?
6   How could Gerald tell that Jan was in difficulty?
7   What had caused her to wake up?
8   What might happen if Gerald moved forward?
9   What do you think Gerald might do next?
10   Do you think that Jan and Gerald can possibly survive?

EXERCISE 11   *Early Risers*

At the top of the bank, close to the wild cherry where the blackbird sang, was a little group of holes almost hidden by brambles. In the green half-light at the mouth of one of these holes, two rabbits were sitting together side by side. At length, the larger of the two came out, slipped along the bank under cover of the brambles and so down into the ditch and up into the field. A few moments later the other followed.

The first rabbit stopped in a sunny patch and scratched his ear with rapid movements of his hind leg. Although he was a yearling and still below his first weight, he had not the harassed look of most 'outskirters' – that is, the rank and file of ordinary rabbits in their first year who, lacking either aristocratic parentage or unusual size and strength, get sat on by their elders and live as best they can – often in the open – on the edge of the warren. He looked as though he knew how to take care of himself. There was a shrewd, buoyant air about him as he sat up, looked round and rubbed both front paws over his nose. As soon as he was satisfied that all was well, he laid back his ears and set to work on the grass.

Richard Adams, *Watership Down*

1 Why was it difficult to see the rabbit holes?
2 Where were the rabbits sitting?
3 Which of the rabbits led the way into the field?
4 Where did the first rabbit stop?
5 How did he scratch his ear?
6 Where do 'outskirters' live?
7 How old are they?
8 In what way was the first rabbit different from most outskirters?
9 Why did he wait so long before starting to eat the grass?
10 How do you think the rabbit had become so confident?

EXERCISE 12 *Gus and the Gang*

Gus knew all the orchards worth scrumping and they raided them for hard green apples which they threw away half-eaten. They fished for newts in Gibbert's Dyke, climbed trees in the woods, kicked an old football about in the recreation ground, traversed the ironwork of the railway bridge over the river and dropped stones into the black greasy depths below. They conducted their first experiments in smoking with the aid of a machine which dispensed a packet containing two Woodbines and two matches for a penny. Or at least, Joby experimented, for it seemed that Gus was already an accomplished smoker who could tackle a cigarette in grown-man fashion without turning a hair. And then Gus and Tommy introduced Joby to an activity so exciting it galvanized him with a tension that seemed to charge his blood with electricity.

Stan Barstow, *Joby*

1 What did the boys do with the apples they stole from the orchards?
2 What did they fish for in Gibbert's Dyke?
3 What did the boys do on the old railway bridge?
4 Where did they obtain their first cigarettes?
5 How much did the packet cost?
6 Why did Joby feel such a novice at smoking?
7 Who introduced Joby to the 'new activities'?
8 How did Joby feel when he was introduced to these activities?
9 What do you think the 'new activities' might have been?
10 How do you think Gus knew all the orchards worth scrumping and was such an accomplished smoker?

EXERCISE 13 The Hungry Toad

The worm performed a particularly convulsive figure of eight, and the toad leant further forward with excitement. Its great mouth opened, the pink tongue flicked out, and the forepart of the worm was carried into the gaping maw. The toad shut its mouth with a snap, and most of the worm, which hung outside, coiled about wildly. The toad sat back and with great care proceeded to stuff the tail end of the worm into its mouth, using its thumbs. As each section of the thrashing worm was pushed in, the toad would gulp hard, closing its eyes with an expression as if of acute pain. Slowly but surely, bit by bit, the worm disappeared between the thick lips, until at last there was only a fraction of an inch dangling outside, twitching to and fro.

'Um,' said Theodore in an amused tone of voice, 'I always like watching them do that. It reminds me of those conjurers, you know, that pull yards and yards of tapes or coloured ribbons out of their mouths ... er ... only, of course, the other way ROUND.'

Gerald Durrell, My Family and Other Animals

1 What shape did the worm make?
2 What colour was the toad's tongue?
3 Which part of the worm did the toad.eat first?
4 What happened to the rest of the worm?
5 What expression did the toad make as it swallowed the worm?
6 How much of the worm was left at the end of the performance?
7 Why did Theodore enjoy the act so much?
8 What was the difference between the action of the toad and a conjurer?
9 Was Theodore right to be so amused at one creature devouring another?
10 Can you think of any other ways in which animals can be entertaining?

EXERCISE 14 *Terror in the Graveyard*

'Hold your noise!' cried a terrible voice, as a man started up from among the graves at the side of the church porch. 'Keep still, you little devil, or I'll cut your throat!'

A fearful man, all in coarse grey, with a great iron on his leg. A man with no hat, and with broken shoes, and with an old rag tied round his head. A man who had been soaked in water, and smothered in mud, and lamed by stones, and cut by flints, and stung by nettles and torn by briars; who limped and shivered, and glared and growled; and whose teeth chattered in his head as he seized me by the chin.

'O! Don't cut my throat, sir,' I pleaded in terror. 'Pray don't do it, sir.'

'Tell us your name!' said the man. 'Quick.'

'Pip, sir.'

'Once more,' said the man, staring at me. 'Give it mouth!'

'Pip. Pip, sir.'

'Show us where you live,' said the man. 'Point out the place!'

I pointed to where our village lay, on the flat in-shore among the alder trees and pollards, a mile or more from the church.

Charles Dickens, *Great Expectations*

1 Where had the man been hiding?
2 What did he have on his leg?
3 What was he wearing on his head?
4 How did Pip know that the man had been hiding in the open for some time?
5 How did the man grab hold of Pip?
6 What did the man want to know?
7 Where was Pip's village situated?
8 How far was it from the church?
9 Who do you think this man was?
10 What do you think happens to Pip?

EXERCISE 15 *A Day Off*

On Sundays there was no work. Breakfast was an hour later than usual, and after breakfast there was a ceremony which was observed every week without fail. First came the hoisting of the flag. Snowball had found in the harness-room an old green tablecloth of Mrs Jones's and had painted on it a hoof and a horn in white. This was run up the flagstaff in the farmhouse garden every Sunday morning. The flag was green, Snowball explained, to represent the green fields of England, while the hoof and horn signified the future Republic of the Animals which would arise when the human race had been finally overthrown. After the hoisting of the flag all the animals trooped into the big barn for a general assembly which was known as the Meeting. Here the work of the coming week was planned out and resolutions were put forward and debated.

George Orwell, *Animal Farm*

1 How was breakfast different on Sundays?
2 How often was the ceremony held?
3 What was the first thing that happened?
4 Where had Snowball found the old tablecloth?
5 How had he changed it into a flag?
6 Why was the flag green?
7 What did the hoof and horn represent?
8 Why do you think animals followed the human custom of not working on Sundays?
9 What happened at the meeting?
10 Do you think that Snowball's plan could ever work?

EXERCISE 16 *Love Letters*

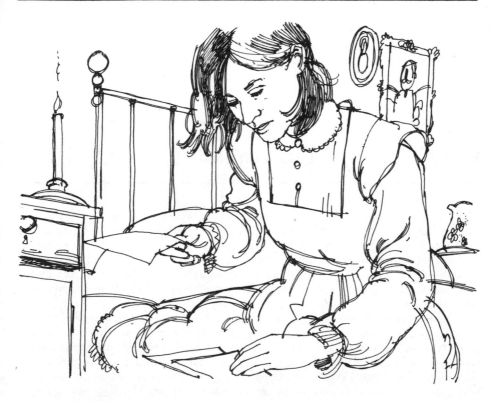

My curiosity and suspicions were roused; I determined to take a look at her mysterious treasures; so, at night, as soon as she and my master were safe upstairs, I searched and readily found among the house keys one that would fit the lock. Having opened, I emptied the whole contents into my apron, and took them with me to examine at leisure in my own chamber.

Though I could not but suspect, I was still surprised to discover that they were a mass of correspondence – daily, almost, it must have been from Linton Heathcliff, answers to documents forwarded by her. The earlier dated were embarrassed and short; gradually, however, they expanded into copious love letters, foolish as the age of the writer rendered natural, yet with touches, here and there, which I thought were borrowed from a more experienced source.

Some of them struck me as singularly odd compounds of ardour and flatness, commencing in strong feeling and concluding in the affected, wordy way that a schoolboy might use to a fancied, incorporeal sweetheart.

Emily Brontë, *Wuthering Heights*

1 When did she choose to examine the treasures?
2 How did she find a key to the lock?
3 Where did she take the articles to examine them?
4 How did she carry them?
5 Why did she take the entire contents of the drawer?
6 What were the 'treasures'?
7 How did the letters change over a period of time?
8 What did she suspect about parts of Heathcliff's letters?
9 Why do you think the girl was so interested in the letters?
10 Do you think that she was disappointed with what she found?

EXERCISE 17 Alone around the World

I went to bed as soon as it was dark, partly to save lights and partly because I was very tired. I was out of the shipping lanes but occasionally still saw ships, so I kept on the masthead light and reduced my watches to an hour. It wasn't really an efficient lookout but I thought, illogically I admit, that as I'd almost been hit once, I was probably all right for a while. I had come to hate the sound of the alarm clock and as a defence would waken myself just before it went off. However, I never trusted myself to wake without it.

The sound of the alarm clock was bad enough, but the off course alarm was worse. It had evil connotations: it not only meant a change of wind direction but the probability of an increase or decrease of wind as well. This, in turn, might mean having to stay up on deck and change sails, and that was an unpleasant prospect in the middle of the night. When the alarm clock went off, however, I would just jump up on deck, take a quick look round and dive back into my sleeping bag again.

Naomi James, *At One with the Sea*

1 Why did Naomi go to bed as soon as it was dark?
2 Why did she keep her masthead light on?
3 Why do you think she reduced the length of her watches?
4 Why did she feel so sure that she would not be struck by another ship?
5 How did she avoid the sound of the alarm clock?
6 When did the off course alarm sound?
7 What did Naomi have to do when the direction and strength of the wind changed?
8 How differently did she react when the ordinary alarm clock went off?
9 Why do you think Naomi and others like her attempt such daring and solitary acts?
10 What do you think she would have missed most?

EXERCISE 18 *Atomic Blast*

Then a tremendous flash of light cut across the sky. Mr Tanimoto has a distinct recollection that it travelled from east to west, from the city towards the hills. It seemed a sheet of sun. Both he and Mr Matsuo reacted in terror – and both had time to react (for they were 3,500 yards, or two miles, from the centre of the explosion). Mr Matsuo dashed up the front steps into his house and dived among the bedrolls and buried himself there. Mr Tanimoto took four or five steps and threw himself between two big rocks in the garden. He bellied up very hard against one of them. As his face was against the stone he did not see what happened. He felt a sudden pressure, and then splinters and pieces of board and fragments of tile fell on him. He heard no roar. (Almost no one in Hiroshima recalls hearing any noise of the bomb but a fisherman in his sampan on the Inland Sea near Tsuzu, the man with whom Mr Tanimoto's mother-in-law and sister-in-law were living, saw the flash and heard a tremendous explosion; he was nearly twenty miles from Hiroshima, but the thunder was greater than when the B29s hit Iwakuni, only five miles away.)

John Hersey, *Hiroshima*

1 In which direction did Mr Tanimoto believe the flash of light had travelled?
2 What did the flash of light resemble?
3 Why did Mr Tanimoto and Mr Matsuo have time to react?
4 Where did they take cover?
5 Why did Mr Tanimoto not see what happened?
6 What happened after he felt the pressure of the blast?
7 Where was the fisherman working when he heard the bomb?
8 How far away from Hiroshima had he been working when the bomb exploded?
9 Why do you think no one on Hiroshima heard the bomb explode?
10 What do you think Mr Tanimoto and Mr Matsuo might have seen when they had recovered from the shock of the blast?

EXERCISE 19 *Conditioning*

The Head Nurse, who was standing by a switchboard at the other end of the room, pressed down a little lever.

There was a violent explosion. Shriller and even shriller, a siren shrieked. Alarm bells maddeningly sounded.

The children started, screamed; their faces were distorted with terror.

'And now,' the Director shouted (for the noise was deafening), 'now we proceed to rub in the lesson with a mild electric shock.'

He waved his hand again, and the Head Nurse pressed a second lever. The screaming of the babies suddenly changed its tone. There was something desperate, almost insane, about the sharp spasmodic yelps to which they now gave utterance. Their little bodies twitched and stiffened; their limbs moved jerkily as if to the tug of unseen wires.

'We can electrify that whole strip of floor,' bawled the Director in explanation. 'But that's enough,' he signalled to the nurse.

Aldous Huxley, *Brave New World*

1 Where was the Head Nurse standing when she pressed down the lever?
2 What sound did the siren make?
3 What happened to the children's faces?
4 How did the Head Nurse know when to press the second lever?
5 What happened to the children's bodies after the second lever had been pressed?
6 Why did the Director have to shout so loudly?
7 How had the Director caused so much suffering?
8 What do you think he may have been trying to prove?
9 How can you tell that this extract is from a story set some time in the future?
10 Do you think that experiments like this may ever be carried out?

EXERCISE 20 The Unseen Stranger

Mary was about to step out into the hall once more and creep past the stairs to the farther passage, when a sound from above made her pause and lift her head. It was the creaking of a board. There was silence for a minute, and then it happened again: quiet footsteps pacing gently overhead. Aunt Patience slept in the farther passage at the other end of the house, and Mary herself had heard Harry the pedlar ride away on his pony nearly ten minutes ago. Her uncle she knew to be in the bar with the stranger, and no one had climbed the stairs since she had descended them. There, the board creaked again, and the soft footsteps continued. Someone was in the empty guest room on the floor above.

Mary's heart began to thump in her side again, and her breath came quickly. Whoever was in hiding up above must have been there many hours. He must have lain in waiting there since the early evening; stood behind the door when she had gone to bed. Had he gone later she would have heard his footsteps on the stairs. Perhaps he had watched the arrival of the wagons from the window as she had done, and had seen the idiot boy run screaming down the road to Dozmary. She had been separated from him by a thin partition of wall, and he must have heard her every movement – the falling on to her bed, and later her dressing, and her opening of her door.

Daphne du Maurier, *Jamaica Inn*

1 What made Mary stop and listen?
2 Where did Aunt Patience sleep?
3 Who was her uncle with?
4 Where did Mary think the noise came from?
5 How did Mary know that Harry the pedlar could not have made the noise?
6 How did Mary guess the person in hiding must have been there for many hours?
7 What strange events had happened at the inn earlier that evening?
8 Why do you think Mary found the unseen visitor's presence so frightening?
9 Who might the visitor be? What could he be doing at the inn that he needed to hide away for so long?
10 What impression of the inn do you get from reading this passage? Write a description of it as you imagine it to be.

EXERCISE 21 *Slipping Away*

'There's two chaps below looking for you,' he whispered. 'They're in the dining-room having whiskies and sodas. They asked about you and said they hoped to meet you here. Oh! and they described you jolly well, down to your boots and shirt. I told them you had been here last night and had gone off on a motor bicycle this morning, and one of the chaps swore like a navvy.'

I made him tell me what they looked like. One was a dark-eyed thin fellow with bushy eyebrows, the other was always smiling and lisped in his talk. Neither was any kind of foreigner; on this my young friend was positive.

I took a bit of paper and wrote these words in German as if they were part of a letter....

'Black Stone. Scudder had got on to this, but he could not act for a fortnight. I doubt if I can do any good now, especially as Karilodes is uncertain about his plans. But if Mr T advises I will do the best I....'

I manufactured it rather neatly, so that it looked like a loose page of a private letter.

'Take this down and say it was found in my bedroom, and ask them to return it to me if they overtake me.'

John Buchan, *The Thirty-nine Steps*

1 How many men were looking for him?
2 Where were the men waiting?
3 How had the waiter misled the men?
4 How did the waiter know that the men were very anxious to see the man?
5 What were the two men like?
6 Why do you think the old man was so certain that neither of the men was a foreigner?
7 What did the man hope would happen as a result of his writing the scribbled note?
8 Where was the waiter to say he had found the note?
9 Why might the two men have been so keen to catch up with the man?
10 Do you think the two men might fall for the trick? What happens next?

EXERCISE 22 Sunday in the Boys' Home

Some things you could be completely certain about on Sundays. There would be a hundred and fifty eggs boiled in a pillowcase and you each got one at breakfast; you also got an individual egg boiled for you on your birthday, unless the cook forgot, in which case you had to wait until the next year.

Another Sunday thing was butter beans and pale cold meat for lunch, and potatoes steamed in their froggy skins. In the afternoon Matron would waddle into the chapel and talk about Jesus and thieving, and keeping clean in mind and body, and how her old boys used to write and say how much they had enjoyed it at Dickie's. With normal luck that was the last we saw of Matron until the following Sunday.

The Gaffer was different. He was always there. His Sunday speciality used to be to warn us of swift and terrible vengeance if anyone was caught reading *News of the World*. This retribution was presumably to come from him, although he intimated that it might easily arrive from God. Anyone found smoking would be struck by lightning.

Leslie Thomas, *This Time Next Week*

1 How did the cook manage to cook so many eggs at once?
2 What happened to your individual egg if cook forgot your birthday?
3 What did the children normally eat for Sunday lunch at Dickie's?
4 What did Matron talk about on Sunday afternoons?
5 What did Matron say the old boys of the school used to write in their letters?
6 How did the Gaffer differ from Matron?
7 What was Gaffer's 'Sunday speciality'?
8 What did the Gaffer suggest would happen to anyone caught smoking?
9 Why do you think the Gaffer considered it such a crime to read the *News of the World*?
10 Do you think that the boys really did enjoy it at Dickie's?

EXERCISE 23 *The Mechanical Attacker*

He turned and the Mechanical Hound was there.

It was half across the lawn, coming from the shadows, moving with such drifting ease that it was like a single solid cloud of black-grey smoke blown at him in silence.

It made a single last leap into the air, coming down at Montag from a good three feet over its head, its spidered legs reaching, the procaine needle snapping out its single angry tooth. Montag caught it with a bloom of fire, a single wondrous blossom that curled in petals of yellow and blue and orange about the metal dog, clad it in a new covering as it slammed into Montag and threw him ten feet back against the bole of a tree, taking the flame gun with him. He felt it scrabble and seize his leg and stab the needle in for a moment before the fire snapped the Hound up in the air, burst its metal bones at the joints and blew out its interior in the single flushing of red colour like a skyrocket fastened to the street.

Ray Bradbury, *Fahrenheit 451*

1 Where was the Mechanical Hound when the man turned?
2 What did the Hound look like as it moved?
3 How high did the Hound leap?
4 What sort of weapon did it have?
5 What effect did the flame gun have on the Hound?
6 What happened to Montag when the Hound fell on him?
7 How did the Hound manage to stab Montag?
8 How was the Hound destroyed?
9 Why do you think the Hound was so determined to kill Montag?
10 What job do you think Montag did, that he happened to have a flame gun in his hand when the Hound attacked him?

EXERCISE 24 The Mysterious Stranger

As he came near, what impressed me first was his clothes. He wore dark trousers of some serge material tucked into tall boots and held at the waist by a wide belt, both of a soft black leather tooled in intricate design. A coat of the same dark material as the trousers was neatly folded and strapped to his saddle roll. His shirt was finespun linen, rich brown in colour. The handkerchief knotted loosely around his throat was black silk. His hat was not the familiar stetson, not the familiar grey or muddy tan. It was a plain black, soft in texture, unlike any hat I had ever seen, with a creased crown and a wide curling brim swept down in front to shield the face.

All trace of newness was long since gone from these things. The dust of distance was beaten into them. They were worn and stained and several neat patches showed on the shirt. Yet a kind of magnificence remained and with it a hint of men and manners alien to my limited boy's experience.

Jack Schaefer, *Shane*

1 What first impressed the boy about the man?
2 What were the man's boots and belt made of?
3 Where did the man keep his coat?
4 What colour was his shirt?
5 What was unusual about the man's hat?
6 Why did the man want his hat brim to shield his face?
7 How did the boy know that the man's clothes were well worn?
8 What did he wear round his neck?
9 What made this man so interesting to the boy?
10 Who do you think this man might be?

EXERCISE 25 Shame

Head bowed and eyes upon the ground, the boy limped towards the steps. He knew there were thirty-eight of them, all rough stone and two yards wide. He had never actually counted them, and he could not say precisely when it was he had decided that there were thirty-eight. But there were, and he knew he was right, because he had been running up and down them more times a day than he could remember for the last seven years.

Today, though, he did not think he would be able to run up the steps. He had been caned by the headmaster that morning, up in B Dormitory, thirteen times and with his pants down. It was still very vivid in his memory.

There had been three of them, all offenders, each beside a bed and waiting for the old man to march in. They had been spotted in the fields the day before, stealing bhuta, which was maize. As the only day scholar in the whole school and, more, the son of the kindergarten teacher, he had been recognized by the villagers.

D.R. Sherman, *Old Mali and the Boy*

1   What were the steps made of?
2   How did the boy know how many steps there were?
3   How long had the boy been living near the school?
4   How many times had he been caned?
5   How many other boys had been punished?
6   What had they all done wrong?
7   Why was it easy for the villagers to identify one boy in particular?
8   Why do you think the punishment was so severe?
9   What other punishment might the headmaster have used?
10 How do you think the boy might explain what had happened to his parents?

With this second boatload came both the captain and the mate. The former was a clumsy great fellow with a sad, silly face. He was bulky; yet so ill-proportioned one got no impression of power. He was modestly dressed in drab shore-going suit: he was newly shaven, and his sparse hair was pomaded so that it lay in a few dark ribbons across his baldish head top. But all this shore-decency of appearance only accentuated his big splodgy brown hands, stained and scarred and corned with his calling. Moreover, instead of boots he wore a pair of gigantic heelless slippers in the Moorish manner, which he must have sliced with a knife out of some pair of dead sea-boots. Even his great spreading feet could hardly keep them on, so that he was obliged to walk at the slowest of shuffles, flop-flop along the deck. He stooped, as if always afraid of banging his head on something; and carried the backs of his hands forward like an orang-utan.

Richard Hughes, *A High Wind in Jamaica*

1 How did the captain and mate arrive on the ship?
2 Why did the captain not appear to be powerful?
3 How had he arranged his hair?
4 Why were the captain's hands 'stained and scarred and corned'?
5 What did the captain wear on his feet?
6 Why did he look so ridiculous?
7 Where might the slippers have come from?
8 Why was the captain forced to walk 'like an orang-utan'?
9 What sort of impression do you think the captain was trying to create?
10 What do you think the captain and mate plan to do?

EXERCISE 27 A World of Change

The world has turned topsy-turvy, respectable people are being sent off to concentration camps, prisons, and lonely cells, and the dregs that remain govern young and old, rich and poor. One person walks into the trap through the black market, a second through helping the Jews or other people who've had to go 'underground'; anyone who isn't a member of the N.S.B. doesn't know what may happen to him from one day to another.

This man is a great loss to us too. The girls can't and aren't allowed to haul along our share of potatoes, so the only thing to do is to eat less. I will tell you how we shall do that; it's certainly not going to make things any pleasanter. Mummy says we shall cut out breakfast altogether, have porridge and bread for lunch, and for supper fried potatoes and possibly once or twice per week vegetables or lettuce, nothing more. We're going to be hungry, but anything is better than being discovered.

Anne Frank, *The Diary of Anne Frank*

1 What is happening to respectable people?
2 What sort of person is left to govern those remaining?
3 How do people get caught?
4 What is life like for anyone who is not a member of the N.S.B.?
5 What are the girls forced to do as a result of losing their share of the potatoes?
6 Why will the family not eat breakfast?
7 What will they eat for supper?
8 Why was it better to be hungry than discovered?
9 Who do you think 'This man' might have been?
10 Why might 'Jews or other people' have had to go 'underground'?

EXERCISE 28 *The Party*

Every Friday five crates of oranges and lemons arrived from a fruiterer in New York –
every Monday these same oranges and lemons left his back door in a pyramid of
pulpless halves. There was a machine in the kitchen which could extract the juice of
two hundred oranges in half an hour if a little button was pressed two hundred times
by a butler's thumb.

At least once a fortnight a corps of caterers came down with several hundred
coloured lights to make a Christmas tree of Gatsby's enormous garden. On buffet
tables, garnished with glistening hors-d'œuvre, spiced baked hams crowded against
salads of harlequin designs and pastry pigs and turkeys bewitched to a dark gold. In
the main hall a bar with a real brass rail was set up, and stocked with gins and liquors
and with cordials so long forgotten that most of his female guests were too young to
know one from the other.

By seven o'clock the whole orchestra has arrived, no thin five-piece affair, but a whole pitful of oboes and trombones and saxophones and viols and cornets and piccolos, and low and high drums. The last swimmers have come in from the beach now and are dressing upstairs; the cars from New York are parked five deep in the drive and already the halls and salons and verandas are gaudy with primary colours and hair bobbed in strange new ways, and shawls beyond the dreams of Castile.

F. Scott Fitzgerald, *The Great Gatsby*

1 Where did the crates of oranges and lemons come from?
2 What happened to the fruit between Friday and Monday?
3 How was the juice extracting machine made to work?
4 How did the caterers make Gatsby's garden into a Christmas tree?
5 Where was the bar set up?
6 What was special about the cordials?
7 Which instruments did the members of the orchestra bring with them?
8 Where were the cars from New York parked?
9 Why do you think parties were held so often?
10 How do we know that these parties were grand, extravagant affairs?

EXERCISE 29 *Accidents Will Happen*

It was Sunday afternoon. The resting horses nibbled the remaining wisps of hay, and they stamped their feet and they bit the wood of the mangers and rattled the halter chains. The afternoon sun sliced in through the cracks of the barn walls and lay in bright lines on the hay. There was the buzz of flies in the air, the lazy afternoon humming.

From outside came the clang of horseshoes on the playing peg and the shouts of men, playing, encouraging, jeering. But in the barn it was quiet and humming and lazy and warm.

Only Lennie was in the barn, and Lennie sat in the hay beside a packing case under a manger in the end of the barn that had not been filled with hay. Lennie sat in the hay and looked at a little dead puppy that lay in front of him. Lennie looked at it for a long time, and then he put out his huge hand and stroked it, stroked it clear from one end to the other.

And Lennie said softly to the puppy: 'Why do you got to get killed? You ain't so little as mice. I didn't bounce you hard.' He bent the pup's head up and looked in its face, and he said to it: 'Now maybe George ain't gonna let me tend no rabbits if he fin's out you got killed.'

He scooped out a little hollow and laid the puppy in it and covered it with hay, out of sight; but he continued to stare at the mound he had made. He said: 'This ain't no bad thing like I got to go hide in the brush. Oh no! This ain't. I'll tell George I found it dead.'

John Steinbeck, *Of Mice and Men*

1   What were the horses eating?
2   What sort of afternoon was it?
3   What game were the men playing outside the barn?
4   Whereabouts in the barn was Lennie sitting?
5   How had Lennie killed the puppy?
6   What had George promised him?
7   Where did he bury the puppy?
8   Where did Lennie usually go when he had done wrong?
9   Why might George not let Lennie keep the rabbits?
10 How do you think George will react to what Lennie has done?

EXERCISE 30 *Granny Trill*

Granny Trill had an original sense of time which seemed to obey some vestigial pattern. She breakfasted, for instance, at four in the morning, had dinner at ten, took tea at two-thirty, and was back in her bed at five. This regime never varied either winter or summer, and belonged very likely to her childhood days when she lived in the woods with her father. To me it seemed a monstrous arrangement, upsetting the roots of order. But Granny Trill's time was for God, or the birds, and although she had a clock she kept it simply for the tick, its hands having dropped off years ago.

In contrast to the subterranean, almost cavernous life which Granny Wallon lived down under, Granny Trill's cottage door was always open and her living-room welcomed us daily. Not that she could have avoided us anyway, for she lay at our nimble mercy. Her cottage was just outside our gate and there were geraniums in pots round the door. Her tiny room opened straight on to the bank and was visible as a last year's bird's nest. Smells of dry linen and tea-caddies filled it, together with the sweeter tang of old flesh.

Laurie Lee, *Cider with Rosie*

1   What time did Granny Trill have breakfast?
2   How had she learned her daily routine?
3   Where had she lived as a child?
4   Why did her routine seem so strange?
5   Why did Granny Trill keep a clock with no hands?
6   What did she keep round her front door?
7   What did Granny Trill's house smell of?
8   How did Granny Trill and Granny Wallon differ?
9   Why could Granny Trill not avoid the children?
10 Why do you think the children were so attracted to her?

EXERCISE 31 Morning Search

When the weather was cold the guards were fairly lenient in the morning, though not in the evening. The prisoners untied their belts, and flung their coats wide open. They advanced five abreast and five guards stood waiting to frisk them. The guards slapped their hands down the belted jackets, ran over the right knee pocket, the only one permitted by regulation, and, reluctant to pull off their gloves, felt any object that puzzled them, asking lazily: 'What's that?'

What was there to look for on a prisoner at the morning muster? A knife? But knives weren't taken out of the camp, they were brought into it. In the morning they had to make certain a prisoner wasn't taking three kilograms of bread with him, meaning to escape with it. There was a time when they were so scared of the two-hundred-gram hunks the prisoners took to eat with their dinner that each of the teams had to make a wooden case for carrying the whole ration, after collecting it, piece by piece, from the men. What they reckoned to gain by this stupidity was beyond imagining. More likely it was just another way of tormenting people, giving them something extra to worry about. It meant taking a nibble at your hunk, making your mark on it, so to say, and then putting it in the case: but anyway the pieces were as alike as two peas, they were all off the same loaf.

Alexander Solzhenitsyn, *One Day in the Life of Ivan Denisovich*

1   What did the prisoners do after they untied their belts?
2   How many guards waited to search them?
3   Why was there only one pocket on the prisoner's clothes?
4   Why were the guards reluctant to take their gloves off to search the prisoners?
5   What were the guards searching for in the mornings?
6   How did the teams carry out their bread rations?
7   Why did the guards introduce this rather pointless method of carrying out food?
8   How did the prisoners identify their own pieces of bread?
9   Why were the prisoners treated more leniently in the mornings?
10 Why did the prisoners try to smuggle knives into the camp?

EXERCISE 32 A New Way of Climbing

Then I was tempted by the wall immediately above, which looked solid enough to use a ladder straight up it. I worked my way across, and brought Dave to me and he went to the foot of the wall itself. We started to get our ladders ready – we had five sections altogether – when one of the most impressive avalanches I have ever seen came off the very summit of Pumori. There was a great cloud of windblown, powder snow, which engulfed across the glacier and seemed about to engulf base camp itself. But we were concentrating on the route in front and, after a struggle with our five ladders, bolted them together. This was a style of climbing I had never undertaken before. Pushing up a thirty-foot ladder from a comparatively narrow snow ledge is no joke. It was just as well we had six Sherpas with us. With all of them pushing and heaving, we finally succeeded in balancing our ladder against the wall; it reached a point about four feet below the top.

With true courtesy, partly because I wanted to get some pictures, I gestured to Dave to have the honour of climbing the ladder first. It was a matter of balancing delicately up it – it was still very unstable. He succeeded in putting in an ice piton about two-thirds of the way up, where it came in close to the ice, fastening the ladder to it with a rope, and, now there was no risk of teetering backwards, climbed more rapidly to the top.

Chris Bonington, *Everest, South West Face*

1   Why was Bonington tempted by the wall immediately above him?
2   How many sections of ladder did they have?
3   Where did the avalanche come from?
4   Why did the climbers find it difficult to use the ladders?
5   Who helped them to push up the ladders?
6   How far from the top did the ladder reach?
7   Why did Bonington invite Dave to climb first?

8 How did Dave make the ladder more secure?
9 Why was the cloud of snow such a threat to the expedition?
10 What are the advantages and disadvantages of climbing with ladders?

EXERCISE 33 A Confession

An old servant was sweeping at the end of the landing. He asked him where was the rector's room and the old servant pointed to the door at the far end and looked after him as he went on to it and knocked.

There was no answer. He knocked again more loudly and his heart jumped when he heard a muffled voice say 'Come in!'

He turned the handle and opened the door and fumbled for the handle of the green baize door inside. He found it and pushed it open and went in.

He saw the rector sitting at a desk writing. There was a skull on the desk and a strange solemn smell in the room like the old leather of chairs.

His heart was beating fast on account of the solemn place he was in and the silence of the room: and he looked at the skull and at the rector's kind-looking face.

'Well, my little man,' said the rector, 'what is it?'

Stephen swallowed down the thing in his throat and said, 'I broke my glasses, sir.'

The rector opened his mouth and said, 'Oh.' Then he smiled and said, 'Well, if we broke our glasses we must write home for a new pair.'

'I wrote home, sir,' said Stephen, 'and Father Arnall said I am not to study till they come.'

'Quite right!' said the rector.

James Joyce, *A Portrait of the Artist as a Young Man*

1 Where was the old servant sweeping?
2 What was the rector doing when Stephen entered the room?
3 What did the room smell like?
4 What was the purpose of the shell on the desk?
5 Why was Stephen's heart beating so fast?
6 What was the purpose of Stephen's visit to the rector?
7 What did the rector tell Stephen to do about his broken glasses?
8 Why had Father Arnall told Stephen not to study until his new glasses arrived?
9 How did the rector try to put Stephen at his ease?
10 Why do you think Stephen felt that it was important to tell the rector about his broken glasses?

EXERCISE 34 *The Dog Fight*

Spitz was a practised fighter. From Spitsbergen through the Arctic, and across Canada and the Barrens, he had held his own with all manner of dogs and achieved mastery over them. Bitter rage was his, but never blind rage. In passion to rend and destroy, he never forgot that his enemy was in like passion to rend and destroy. He never rushed till he was prepared to receive a rush; never attacked till he had first defended that attack.

In vain Buck strove to sink his teeth in the neck of the big white dog. Wherever his fangs struck for the softer flesh, they were countered by the fangs of Spitz. Fang clashed fang, and lips were cut and bleeding, but Buck could not penetrate his enemy's guard. Then he warmed up and enveloped Spitz in a whirlwind of rushes. Time and time again he tried for the snow-white throat, where life bubbled near the surface, and each time and every time Spitz slashed him and got away. Then Buck took to rushing, as though for the throat, when, suddenly drawing back his head and curving in from side to side, he would drive his shoulder at the shoulder of Spitz, as a ram by which to overthrow him. But instead, Buck's shoulder was slashed down each time as Spitz leapt lightly away.

Spitz was untouched, while Buck was streaming with blood and panting hard. The fight was growing desperate. And all the while the silent and wolfish circle waited to finish off whichever dog went down. As Buck grew winded, Spitz took to rushing and he kept him staggering for footing. Once Buck went over, and the whole circle of sixty dogs started up; but he recovered himself, almost in mid-air, and the circle sank down again and waited.

Jack London, *Call of the Wild*

35

1 Where had Spitz learned how to fight?
2 In what ways was he a cunning fighter?
3 Why was Buck unable to break through Spitz's guard?
4 Why did Buck aim for Spitz's throat?
5 When did Buck start to rush Spitz?
6 Why did he charge at Spitz's shoulder?
7 How many dogs were waiting to see the result of the fight?
8 What were they waiting for?
9 How do you think the fight started?
10 Which dog do you think is more likely to win the fight?

EXERCISE 35 The Letter

'I think I'd better dress that knee for you, Leo. It's looking a bit messy.'

Glad to get away, I followed her. She went to the bathroom: it was the only one, I think, in the whole house. I had never seen it before: Marcus and I had a round bath in our room.

'Stay here,' she ordered, 'and I'll find you another bandage.'

It was a big room with, which seemed to me unnecessary, a wash-stand in it: for why should people want to have a bath and wash as well? The bath was encased in mahogany and had a mahogany lid. It looked like a tomb. When she came back she lifted the lid and made me sit on the edge of the bath while she took my shoe and stocking off, as if she didn't know that I was old enough to do it for myself. 'Now put your knee under the tap,' she said.

The water trickled down my leg deliciously cool.

'My goodness,' she said, 'you did come a cropper,' but to my surprise she said nothing about Ted Burgess until almost the end, after she had put on the new bandage. The old one was lying on the edge of the bath, all creased and blood-stained, and she looked at it and said, 'Is that his handkerchief?'

'Yes,' I said. 'He said he wouldn't want it back, so shall I throw it away? I know where the rubbish tip is' – it wasn't officiousness, I wanted to save her the trouble. And I welcomed the chance to revisit the rubbish heap, that grateful touch of squalor in all the magnificence.

Then I remembered the letter, which I had kept forgetting, for while I was with her I only thought about her. 'He asked me to give you this,' I said, pulling it out of my pocket. 'I'm afraid it's rather crumpled.'

L.P. Hartley, *The Go-Between*

1 Why was this the first time that Leo had seen the bathroom?
2 Why did he consider it unnecessary to have a wash-stand in the bathroom?
3 Why did the bath look like a tomb?

4   Why did Leo put his knee under the tap?
5   To whom did the handkerchief belong?
6   Why did Leo want to throw the handkerchief away?
7   Why was the rubbish tip so attractive?
8   Why had Leo forgotten to give her the letter?
9   What do you think the letter said?
10   How do you think Leo might have acquired the letter?

EXERCISE 36 *Depth~charge*

Someone on the bridge said, 'Any minute now....'
   The U-boat rose in their wake like a huge unwieldy fish, black and gleaming in the sunlight.
   A great roar went up from the men on the upper deck, a howl of triumph. The U-boat came up bows first at an extraordinary angle, blown right out of her proper trim by the force of the explosion: clearly she was, for the moment, beyond control. The water sluiced and poured from her casings as she rose: great bubbles burst round her conning-tower: gouts of oil spread outwards from the crushed plating amidships. 'Open fire!' shouted Ericson – and for a few moments it was Baker's chance, and his alone: the two-pounder pom-pom, set just behind the funnel, was the only gun that could be brought to bear. The staccato force of its firing shook the still air, and with a noise and a chain of shock like the punch! punch! punch! of a trip-hammer the red glowing tracer-shells began to chase each other across the water towards the U-boat. She had now fallen back on a level keel, and for the moment she rode at her proper trim: it was odd, and infinitely disgusting, suddenly to see this wicked object, the loathsome cause of a hundred nights of fear and disaster, so close to them, so innocently exposed. It was like seeing some criminal, who had outraged honour and society, and had long been shunned, taking his ease at one's own fireside.

Nicholas Monsarrat, *The Cruel Sea*

1   What did the U-boat look like as it surfaced?
2   How did the men on the upper deck react to its appearance?
3   What caused the U-boat to surface at an odd angle?
4   Where did the gouts of oil come from?
5   Where was the pom-pom gun located on the ship?
6   Why was Baker's gun the only one to fire at the submarine?
7   How did the firing of the gun resemble the noise of a trip-hammer?
8   For how long had the ship been hunting the U-boat?
9   Why was Ericson so disgusted by the appearance of the U-boat?
10   Do you think Ericson was right to open fire at the U-boat without giving her captain the chance to surrender?

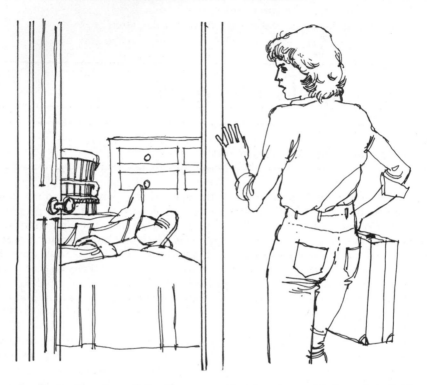

Frances waited a long time. John Henry was sleeping across the foot of the bed, still dressed and with his shoes on, and his mouth was open and one ear of his glasses frame had come loose. After waiting as long as she could stand it, she took the suitcase and tiptoed very quietly down the stairs. It was dark down there, dark in her father's room, dark through the house. She stood on the threshold of her father's room and he was snoring softly. The hardest time was the few minutes she stood there, listening.

The rest was easy. Her father was a widowman, set in his ways, and at night he folded his pants over a straight chair and left his wallet, watch, and glasses on the right-hand side of the bureau. She moved very quietly in the darkness and laid hands on the wallet almost immediately. She was careful opening the bureau drawer, stopping to listen each time there was a scraping sound. The pistol felt heavy and cool in her hot hand. It was easy except for the loudness of her beating heart and for an accident that happened just as she crept from the room. She stumbled over a wastepaper basket and the snoring stopped. Her father stirred, muttered. She held her breath – then finally, after a minute, the snoring went on again.

Carson McCullers, *The Member of the Wedding*

1 Where was John Henry sleeping?
2 What did Frances carry down the stairs with her?
3 When was the most difficult time for her?
4 How did Frances know where to find her father's wallet?
5 Why did she need to be so careful opening the drawer?
6 What did the pistol feel like in her hand?
7 How did Frances nearly wake her father?
8 How long did she have to wait before she could move again?
9 Why do you think John Henry was asleep fully clothed?
10 Why do you think Frances was leaving home with a stolen pistol and wallet?

EXERCISE 38 *Maria's Excitement*

About the middle of the next day, as she was in her room getting ready for a walk, a sudden noise below seemed to speak to the whole house in confusion; and, after listening a moment, she heard somebody running upstairs in a violent hurry, and calling loudly after her. She opened the door and met Maria in the landing place, who, breathless with agitation, cried out, 'Oh, my dear Eliza! pray make haste and come into the dining-room, for there is such a sight to be seen! I will not tell you what it is. Make haste, and come down this moment.'

Elizabeth asked questions in vain; Maria would tell her nothing more, and down they ran into the dining-room, which fronted the lane, in quest of this wonder; it was two ladies stopping in a low phaeton at the garden gate.

'And is this all?' cried Elizabeth. 'I expected at least that the pigs were got into the garden, and here is nothing but Lady Catherine and her daughter!'

'La! my dear,' said Maria, quite shocked at the mistake, 'it is not Lady Catherine. The old lady is Mrs Jenkinson, who lives with them; the other is Miss de Bourgh. Only look at her. She is quite a little creature. Who would have thought she could be so thin and small!'

Jane Austen, *Pride and Prejudice*

1 What was Elizabeth doing when she heard the noise?
2 Where did the noise come from?
3 Where did she meet Maria?
4 How could Elizabeth tell that Maria was very excited?
5 Why did Maria not answer any of Elizabeth's questions?
6 What did Elizabeth see from the dining-room?
7 Why was Elizabeth disappointed?
8 Why was Maria so shocked at what Elizabeth had said?
9 Why do you think Maria was so agitated by what she had seen?
10 Why was Miss de Bourgh so disappointing?

EXERCISE 39 *The Prison Camp*

The child nodded and went off. Jean went back to the veranda and waited; presently the Chinaman appeared carrying a tray loaded with little tubes and pots. He approached the sentry and spoke to him, indicating his wish to sell his wares; after some hesitation the sentry agreed. Jean got six tubes of repellant and the rest was swiftly taken by the other women. Halijah got ten cents.

Presently a Japanese orderly brought two buckets of a thin fish soup and another half full of boiled rice, dirty and unappetizing. There were no bowls or utensils to eat with. There was nothing to be done but to eat as best they could; at that time they had not fallen into the prisoner's mode of life in which all food is shared out and divided scrupulously, so that some got much more than others, who got little or none. There were still food supplies, however, so they fell back on the biscuits and the private stocks to supplement the ration.

That afternoon the men were separated from their families, and marched off under guard. Bill Holland turned from his fat, motherly wife, his eyes moist. 'Goodbye, Jean,' he said heavily. 'Good luck.' And then he said, 'Stick with them, if you can, won't you?'

She nodded. 'I'll do that. We'll all be in the same camp together.'

The men were formed up together, seven of them, and marched off under guard.

Nevil Shute, *A Town Like Alice*

1   Where did Jean wait?
2   What did the Chinaman carry on his tray?
3   What do you think he said to the sentry?
4   What did Jean buy?

5   Why was the food so unappetizing?
6   How did the prisoners eat their food?
7   Why did some receive more food than others?
8   What did Bill Holland want his wife to do?
9   Why do you think the sentry was hesitant in allowing the Chinaman to sell his
     goods?
10   Why were the Japanese separating the men from the women?

EXERCISE 40 *Dreams of the Future*

Eating oranges in St Botolph's churchyard on the long crisp nights, or sometimes in
the public shelter at the Corporation cemetery, another favourite spot, we had
discussed at length the prospect of living in a thatched cottage in the middle of some
unspecified field in Devon. At times, in the right mood, I could get enthusiastic over
this rural image, and it had even figured in my No. 1 thinking before now. We had
invented two children, little Barbara and little Billy – the prototypes, actually, of the
imaginary family I had told Arthur's mother about – and we would discuss their
future, and the village activities, and the poker-work mottoes and all the rest of it.
   'It's sort of turquoise, with lovely little squiggles, like wineglasses ...'
   'Will it go with the yellow carpet?'
   'No, but it'll go with the grey rugs in the kiddies' room'
   'Dalling!'
   The yellow carpet and the grey rugs we had seen in a furniture shop window on one
of the interminable expeditions round Stradhoughton that the Witch sometimes
dragged me on. They had all long ago been sold, but many had become part of the
picture of our cottage, along with the Windsor chairs, the kettle singing on the hob,
the cat, and also the crinoline ladies from my bedroom wall at home.

                                        Keith Waterhouse, *Billy Liar*

1   In which season of the year did Billy and Barbara meet in the churchyard and
     cemetery?
2   Where was the public shelter situated?
3   When did Billy enjoy thinking about the dream cottage in Devon?
4   What colour were the rugs in the 'kiddies' room' in their imaginary home?
5   Where had they seen the furnishings for their home?
6   What nickname did Billy have for Barbara?
7   Do you think that Billy enjoyed the shopping expeditions?
8   How did Barbara complete the dream picture of their cottage?
9   Were Billy and Barbara well suited to each other?
10   Do you think they could ever realize their dreams and one day live together in
     their imaginary home?

EXERCISE 41 The New Teacher

Miss Caroline Fisher, our teacher, was no more than twenty-one. She had bright auburn hair, pink cheeks, and wore crimson finger-nail polish. She also wore high-heeled pumps and a red-and-white striped dress. She looked and smelled like a peppermint drop. She boarded across the street one door down from us in Miss Maudie Atkinson's upstairs front room, and when Miss Audie introduced us to her, Jem was in a haze for days.

Miss Caroline printed her name on the blackboard and said, 'This says I am Miss Caroline Fisher. I am from North Alabama.' The class murmured apprehensively, should she prove to harbour her share of the peculiarities indigenous to that region.

Miss Caroline began the day by reading a story about cats. The cats had long conversations with one another, they wore cunning little clothes and lived in a warm room beneath a kitchen stove. By the time Mrs Cat called the drugstore for an order of chocolate mice the class was wriggling like a bucketful of worms.

Harper Lee, *To Kill a Mockingbird*

1   How old was Miss Caroline Fisher?
2   Why did she look and smell like a 'peppermint drop'?
3   Where was Miss Caroline staying whilst she taught at the school?
4   What effect did she have on Jem?

5 Which part of the United States did Miss Caroline come from?
6 How did she introduce herself to the class?
7 How did she begin her first lesson of the day?
8 What was her story about?
9 Why do you think the class began 'wriggling like a bucketful of worms'?
10 What do you think the class thought of Miss Caroline after her first day's teaching?

EXERCISE 42 *Hiding in the Crowds*

Hale knew, before he had been in Brighton three hours, that they meant to murder him. With his inky fingers and his bitten nails, his manner cynical and nervous, anybody could tell he didn't belong – belong to the early summer sun, the cool Whitsun wind off the sea, the holiday crowd. They came in by train from Victoria every five minutes, rocked down Queen's Road standing on the tops of the little local trams, stepped off in bewildered multitudes into fresh and glittering air: the new silver paint sparkled on the piers, the cream houses ran away into the west like a pale Victorian watercolour; a race in miniature motors, a band playing, flower gardens in bloom below the front, an aeroplane advertising something for the health in pale vanishing clouds across the sky.

It had seemed quite easy to Hale to be lost in Brighton. Fifty thousand people besides himself were down for the day, and for quite a while he gave himself up to the good day, drinking gins and tonics wherever his programme allowed. For he had to stick closely to a programme: from ten till eleven Queen's Road and Castle Square, from eleven till twelve the Aquarium and Palace Pier, twelve till one the front between the Old Ship and West Pier, back for lunch between one and two in any restaurant he chose round the Castle Square, and after that he had to make his way all the way down the parade to the West Pier and then to the station by the Hove streets. These were the limits of his absurd and widely advertised sentry-go.

Graham Greene, *Brighton Rock*

1 How long did it take Hale to realize that the gang meant to kill him?
2 How did his hands reveal his nervous manner?
3 Where did most of the holiday-makers come from?
4 How did they travel down Queen's Road?
5 Where was the flower garden situated?
6 Where did Hale have to go between eleven and twelve o'clock?
7 Why did Hale believe it would be easy to avoid being caught in Brighton?
8 What was the last thing Hale had to do in his daily programme?
9 What was Hale's job?
10 Why do you think a gang might want to kill him?

EXERCISE 43 *Taking a Breather*

Our stopping-place was a store on the river-bank. Behind it there was a small ferry-boat.

We dismounted and tied up our horses. My legs were tingling and weak and I tottered a little as I walked. Nothing can take the starch out of you like a long ride on horseback.

A black mule was tied up to the porch of the store. He had a cotton rope round his neck right under his jaw. The sun had caused the wet rope to draw up tight and the mule was gasping and choking for breath. The more he tugged the worse he made it. Two wicked boys were sitting on the edge of the porch laughing at the mule's discomfort. One was white and the other was an Indian. They were about seventeen years of age.

Rooster cut the rope with his dirk knife and the mule breathed easy again. The grateful beast wandered off shaking his head about. A cypress stump served for a step up to the porch. Rooster went up first and walked over to the two boys and kicked them off into the mud with the flat of his boot.

'Call that sport, do you?' he said. They were two mighty surprised boys.

The storekeeper was a man named Bagby with an Indian wife. They had already had dinner but the woman warmed up some catfish for us that she had left over. Laboeuf and I sat at a table near the stove and ate while Rooster had a conference with the man Bagby at the back of the store.

Charles Portis, *True Grit*

1 Where was the store situated?
2 Why was the girl so tired?
3 Why was the rope on the mule's neck becoming so tight?
4 How old were the two boys watching the mule?
5 How did Rooster release the mule?
6 How did Rooster show how angry he was with the boys?
7 What did the Indian woman give them for their dinner?
8 Why did Rooster not eat his dinner with Laboeuf and the girl?
9 What do you think Rooster might have been asking Bagby?
10 How do you think the storekeeper and his family made a living?

EXERCISE 44 *The Line-up*

Told to go, I trotted down the pavilion steps, out on to the field because the big cross-country was about to begin and the two entries from Gunthorpe had fixed themselves early at the starting-line and were ready to move off like white kangaroos. The sports ground looked a treat; with big tea tents all round and flags flying and seats for the families – empty because no mam or dad had known what opening day meant – and boys still running heats for the hundred yards, and lords and ladies walking from stall to stall, and the Borstal Boys' Brass Band in blue uniforms; and up on the stands the brown jackets of Hucknall as well as our own grey blazers, and then the Gunthorpe lot with shirt-sleeves rolled. The blue sky was full of sunshine and it couldn't have been a better day, and all of the big show was like something out of *Ivanhoe* that we'd seen on the pictures a few days before.

'Come on, Smith,' Roach the sports master called to me, 'we don't want you to be late for the big race, eh? Although I dare say you'd catch them up if you were.' The others cat-called and grunted at this, but I took no notice and placed myself between Gunthorpe and one of the Aylesham trusties, dropped on my knees and plucked a few grass blades to suck on the way round.

Alan Sillitoe, *The Loneliness of the Long Distance Runner*

1　How many runners from Gunthorpe were there?
2　What did the sports ground look like?
3　Why were all the seats empty?
4　What colour were the uniforms of the Brass Band?
5　Why did the scene remind Smith of a scene from *Ivanhoe*?
6　What did Mr Roach think of Smith's skill as a runner?
7　How did the uniforms of the three establishments differ?
8　What did the rest of Smith's class think of Mr Roach's comments?
9　Why do you think Mr Roach was so keen that Smith should win?
10　Do you think it matters to Smith whether he wins or not?

EXERCISE 45 *Incident at the Border*

Leamas watched Karl lean his bicycle against the railing, walk casually to the Customs hut. Don't overdo it, he thought. At last Karl came out, waved cheerfully to the man on the barrier, and the red-and-white pole swung slowly upwards. He was through, he was coming towards them, he had made it. Only the Vopo in the middle of the road, the line and safety.

At that moment Karl seemed to hear some sound, sense danger; he glanced over his shoulder, began to pedal furiously, bending low over the handlebars. There was still the lonely sentry on the bridge, and he had turned and was watching Karl. Then, totally unexpected, the searchlights went on, white and brilliant, catching Karl and holding him in their beam like a rabbit in the headlights of a car. There came the see-saw wail of a siren, the sound or orders wildly shouted. In front of Leamas, the two policemen dropped to their knees, peering through the sandbagged slits, deftly flicking the rapid load on their automatic rifles.

The East German sentry fired, quite carefully, away from them into his own sector. The first shot seemed to thrust Karl forward, the second to pull him back. Somehow he was still moving, still on the bicycle, passing the sentry, and the sentry was still shooting at him. Then he sagged, rolled to the ground, and they heard quite clearly the clatter of the bike as it fell. Leamas hoped to God he was dead.

John le Carré, *The Spy Who Came in from the Cold*

1   Where did Karl lean his bicycle?
2   What was the red-and-white pole used for?
3   Why was Leamas worried as Karl walked up to the Customs hut?
4   Why did Karl start to pedal so hard?
5   Who was guarding the bridge?
6   What effect did the searchlights have?
7   What noise did the siren make?
8   What happened to Karl as he was struck by the bullets fired by the sentry?
9   Why was Karl's escape so important to Leamas?
10   Why does Leamas now hope that Karl is dead?

EXERCISE 46 *The Loss of the Flock*

The experienced ear of Oak knew the sound he now heard to be caused by the running of the flock with great velocity.

He jumped out of bed, dressed, tore down the lane through a foggy dawn, and ascended the hill. The forward ewes were kept apart from those among which the fall of lambs would be later, there being two hundred of the latter class in Gabriel's flock. These two hundred seemed to have absolutely vanished from the hill. There were the fifty with their lambs, enclosed at the other end as he had left them, but the rest, forming the bulk of the flock, were nowhere. Gabriel called at the top of his voice the shepherd's call, 'Ovey, ovey, ovey!'

Not a single bleat. He went to the hedge; a gap had been broken through it, and in the gap were the footprints of the sheep. Rather surprised to find them break fence at this season, yet putting it down instantly to their great fondness for ivy in winter-time, of which a great deal grew in the plantation, he followed through the hedge. They were not in the plantation.

Thomas Hardy, *Far from the Madding Crowd*

1 How did Oak identify the sound of the running flock so easily?
2 What was the weather like that morning?
3 How many ewes had already had their lambs?
4 Where did Oak keep these ewes and their lambs?
5 Why do you think Oak kept them apart from the rest?
6 Where should most of the sheep have been?
7 What did Oak notice in the gap in the hedge?
8 What did Oak believe the sheep were after when they had broken fence?
9 What do you think had happened to the flock?
10 What do you think Oak will do next?

EXERCISE 47 The Lonely Farmhouse

On the edge of Witton Moor they found what John had been looking for – a small farmhouse, compact and isolated. It stood on a slight rise, surrounded by potato fields. There was smoke rising from the chimney. For a moment that puzzled him, until he remembered that, in a remote spot like this, they would probably need a coal fire, even in summer, for cooking. He gave Pirrie his instructions. Pirrie nodded, and rubbed three fingers of his right hand along his nose; he had made the same gesture, John remembered now, before going out after the gang who had taken Ann and Mary.

With Roger, John walked up to the farmhouse. They made no attempt at concealment, and strolled casually as though motivated by idle curiosity. John saw a curtain in one of the front windows twitch, but there was no other sign that they had been observed. An old dog sunned himself against the side of the house. Pebbles crunched under their feet, a casual and friendly sound.

There was a knocker on the door, shaped like a ram's head. John lifted it and dropped it again heavily; it clanged dully against its metal base. As they heard the tread of feet on the other side, the two men stepped a little to the right.

John Christopher, The Death of Grass

1 Where did they find the small farmhouse?
2 How did they know that there were people in the farmhouse?
3 Why might a coal fire still be needed in summer?
4 What did Pirrie do when he had received John's instructions?
5 Why did they approach the house so casually?
6 How did they know that they had been spotted from the house?
7 What was the door knocker shaped like?
8 What did the two men do when they heard footsteps on the other side of the door?
9 What do you think John said to Pirrie before they approached the house?
10 What do you think John intended to do once he was inside the farmhouse?

50

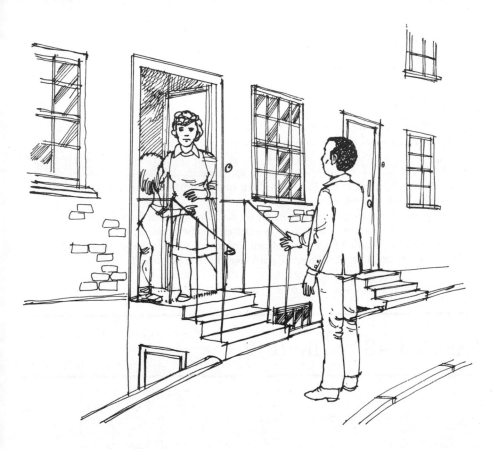

The address was one of a terrace in a rather dingy street, but the pavement outside the front door was, like its neighbour's, scrubbed white, and the brass door knocker and lace window curtains bore testimony to the occupant's attention to cleanliness. Some of these local folk were as house-proud as duchesses. I knocked and presently the door was opened by a large red-faced smiling woman.

'Good evening. I'm here to inquire about the room.'

Immediately the smile was replaced by the expression of cold withdrawal I had come to know so well.

'Sorry, I'm not letting.'

'Mr Pinkus told me about it a few moments ago,' I persisted.

'Sorry, I've changed me mind.' Her arms were folded across her stomach and the set face and bulk of her added to the finality of her words.

51

'Who's it, Mum?' a girlish voice inquired from somewhere behind her.

'Some darky here asking about the room.' Her mouth spat out the words as if each one was intended to revile.

Embarrassed to the point of anger, I was turning away when there was a sudden movement behind her and a voice cried in consternation, 'Oh Gawd, Mum, it's me teacher.' Beside the woman's surprised face I caught a glimpse of the startled, freckled countenance of Barbara Pegg.

E.R. Braithwaite, *To Sir with Love*

1　In what sort of street was the house situated?
2　How did the man know that the occupants of the houses took pride in the cleanliness of their homes?
3　What did the woman who opened the door look like?
4　What was the purpose of the man's visit?
5　How had he found out about the vacant room?
6　How did the man know that Mrs Pegg had definitely made up her mind not to let him have the room?
7　How did the man feel as he turned to walk away from Mrs Pegg?
8　Why was Barbara so shocked at what her mother had said?
9　Why do you think Mrs Pegg did not want the man to have the room?
10　Do you think that Mrs Pegg might now change her mind?

EXERCISE 49 *Pay-day*

'He's here. Where is he? Morel's lad?'

The fat, red, bald little man peered round with keen eyes. He pointed at the fireplace. The colliers looked round, moved aside, and disclosed the boy.

'Here he is,' said Mr Winterbottom.

Paul went to the counter.

'Seventeen pounds eleven and fivepence. Why don't you shout up when you're called?' said Mr Braithwaite. He banged on to the invoice a five-pound bag of silver, then in a delicate and pretty movement, picked up a little ten-pound column of gold, and plumped it beside the silver. The gold slid in a bright stream over the paper. The cashier finished counting off the money; the boy dragged the whole down the counter to Mr Winterbottom, to whom the stoppages for rent and tools must be paid. Here he suffered again.

'Sixteen an' six,' said Mr Winterbottom.

The lad was much too upset to count. He pushed forward some loose silver and half a sovereign.

'How much do you think you've given me?' asked Mr Winterbottom
The boy looked at him, but said nothing. He had not the faintest notion.

D.H. Lawrence, Sons and Lovers

1 What did Mr Braithwaite look like?
2 Where was the boy hiding?
3 How much had Morel earned that week?
4 Why was Mr Braithwaite so angry with the boy?
5 Why did the boy have to pay some money to Mr Winterbottom?
6 Why did the boy not bother to count out the mony for Mr Winterbottom?
7 Why did the boy become so upset during the collection of the wages?
8 What was Morel's job?
9 Why do you think he had not turned up to collect his wages himself?
10 Why do you think the boy was reluctant to 'shout up' to collect the wages?

EXERCISE 50 *Morning Assembly*

'Hymn number one-seven-five, "New Every Morning Is the Love".'

The navy-blue covers of the hymn books, inconspicuous against the dark shades of the boys' clothing, bloomed white across the hall as they were opened and the pages flicked through. The scuff and tick of the turning pages was slowly drowned under a rising chorus of coughing and hawking; until Mr Gryce, furious behind the lectern, scooped up his stick and began to smack it vertically down the face.

'STOP THAT INFERNAL COUGHING.'

The sight and swishsmack of the stick stopped the throat noises of the boys, and the teachers, posted at regular intervals at the ends of the rows, all looked up at the platform. Gryce was straining over the top of the lectern like a bulldog up on its hind legs.

'It's every morning alike. As soon as the hymn is announced you're off revving up. Hm-hmm! Hm-hmm! It's more like a race-track in here than an assembly hall' – hall – ringing across the hall, striking the windows and lingering there like the vibrations of a tuning-fork.

No one muffed. Not a foot scraped. Not a page stirred. The teachers looked seriously into the ranks of boys. The boys stood looking up at Gryce, each one convinced that Gryce was looking at him.

Barry Hines, *A Kestrel for a Knave*

1   What was the title of the hymn the boys were asked to sing?
2   Why did the white pages of the hymn books stand out so clearly?
3   Where was Mr Gryce standing during the assembly?
4   What made him so angry?
5   Why did the boys stop coughing?
6   What did Mr Gryce look like as he shouted at the boys?
7   Why did Mr Gryce compare the assembly hall to a race-track?
8   Where were the teachers standing during the assembly?
9   Why do you think both boys and teachers seemed afraid of Mr Gryce?
10   Why were the boys always so noisy at that time in the assembly?